Writing 4

Descriptive ✓
Expository ✓
Narrative ✓
Persuasive ✓

NARRATIVE
Writing

D1220607

by EMILY HUTCHINSON

—— *Writing* 4 TITLES ——

Descriptive Writing
Expository Writing
Narrative Writing
Persuasive Writing

Development and Production: Laurel Associates, Inc.
Cover Design: Image Quest, Inc.

SADDLEBACK
EDUCATIONAL PUBLISHING

Three Watson
Irvine, CA 92618-2767
Website: www.sdlback.com

ISBN-13: 978-1-56254-752-3
ISBN-10: 1-56254-752-6
eBook: 978-1-60291-543-5

Printed in the United States of America
12 11 10 09 08   9 8 7 6 5 4 3

Contents

To the Student

*How about it?
Can you count on your
writing skills to make
your meaning clear?*

*Check yourself out
by answering the
following questions!*

▶ Can you give other people easy-to-follow directions and explanations?

EXAMPLES: **how to tape a TV show**
how a bill becomes law

▶ Can you describe something clearly enough to create a vivid image in the minds of your audience?

EXAMPLES: **a dramatic thunderstorm**
a movie star's mansion

▶ Can you tell a story so well that your audience is fascinated from beginning to end?

EXAMPLES: **the history of baseball**
the world's worst date

▶ Can you usually persuade others to accept your opinion or take some kind of action?

EXAMPLES: **see a certain movie**
register to vote

Saddleback's WRITING 4 series will improve your written work—no matter what your purpose is for writing. If you make your best effort, the result will surprise you. You'll discover that putting words on paper isn't that much different from saying words out loud. The thought processes and grammatical structures are the same. Writing is just another form of expression; skill develops with practice!

Competent writers do better at school and at work. Keep that in mind as you work your way through these books. If you learn to write well, you're more likely to succeed in whatever you want to do!

Are you ready to go for it?
Follow me—I'm off and running!

Lesson 1 — Friendly Letter

When you write a narrative, you are telling a story. Who's a better audience for your story than a friend? One way we tell our friends stories is by writing letters. Good topics for letters include the interesting things that happen to us during the day.

A. In your letter to a friend, elaborate on this sentence: "You won't believe what happened today!"

Before you begin your letter, write some notes, using the 5Ws + H formula (who, what, when, where, why, and how).

WHO? (Who was involved? Did you see or talk to someone you know personally, someone you know by reputation, or a stranger? Describe the person.)

_____

_____

WHAT? (What happened? What did the person say or do? What did you say or do?)

_____

_____

WHEN? (When did this happen? Describe the time of day.)

_____

_____

WHERE? (Where were you? Where was the other person? Describe the setting.)

_____

_____

WHY? (What caused the event? Tell the reasons why the event happened.)

_____

_____

HOW? (How did you react? How did the other person react? How did the situation get resolved?) _____

_____

_____

B. Now, use the notes you wrote in Part A to help you write a friendly letter. Because you're writing to a friend, make sure your tone is friendly, too. Follow these tips:

- Include details that your friend would understand, appreciate, and enjoy.

- Use figurative language (such as similes, metaphors, hyperbole, irony, or personification) to describe characters and settings. (If you've forgotten what these words mean, look them up in a dictionary.)

- Use the proper form for a friendly letter. Include the date in the upper right area of the letter. Use a friendly greeting followed by a comma and a friendly closing followed by a comma.

(YOUR SIGNATURE)

Lesson 2 — Everyday Experiences

Normal, daily happenings can be a good source of ideas for narrative writing. With enough detail and colorful description, even ordinary events can be made to sound interesting. For example, a visit to a grocery store might be commonplace to you. To a baby, however, it's a new experience full of bright colors, lights, people, sounds, aromas, and products. A visitor from another country might also find an American grocery store quite exotic. Point of view makes all the difference.

A. In what way might each of the following characters experience the circumstances described? Write a sentence that expresses the character's unique point of view. This first one has been done as an example.

1. A four-year-old goes to her first professional baseball game with her father.

   Daddy and I had fun at the ball game. We cheered for our team and ate lots of yummy treats.

2. A young father takes his four-year-old to her first professional baseball game.

   _____

   _____

3. A rookie steps up to the plate for his first at-bat in a professional baseball game.

   _____

   _____

4. The pitcher reacts as the rookie hits a home run.

   _____

   _____

5. The outfielder reacts as the ball sails over his head and into the stands.

   _____

   _____

6. A fan in the bleachers catches the home run ball.

   _____

   _____

7. The four-year-old girl tastes her first cotton candy.

   _____

   _____

B. Now choose an everyday experience that is familiar to you. Write about it from six different points of view. This means trying to imagine the experience as seen through other people's eyes. Ask yourself how the same sights, sounds, aromas, and tastes might seem different to different people. The answer to this will give you ideas for your writing.

Everyday experience: _____

1. **from** _____**'s point of view**

   _____

   _____

2. **from** _____**'s point of view**

   _____

   _____

3. **from** _____**'s point of view**

   _____

   _____

4. **from** _____**'s point of view**

   _____

   _____

5. **from** _____**'s point of view**

   _____

   _____

6. **from** _____**'s point of view**

   _____

   _____

What Happened Next?

Most narratives are told in chronological order (the order in which the events occur). A good example is the narrative poem "Paul Revere's Ride" by Henry Wadsworth Longfellow. In this poem, the narrator tells the story of "the midnight ride of Paul Revere" from start to finish.

A. Read the excerpt from the poem. Notice that even the slightest actions are told in chronological order. Now *you* follow Longfellow's example as you write about a historical event. Use one of the examples below, or choose some other event that interests you.

> Then he climbed the tower of the
> Old North Church,
> By the wooden stairs, with stealthy tread,
> To the belfry-chamber overhead,
> And startled the pigeons from their perch
> On the somber rafters, that round him made
> Masses and moving shapes of shade,—
> By the trembling ladder, steep and tall,
> To the highest window in the wall,
> Where he paused to listen and look down
> A moment on the roofs of the town,
> And the moonlight flowing over all.

Make sure you retell the story in sequence—first things first, followed by the rest. Before you begin, make some notes on the event you will cover.

- the landing of the *Mayflower*
- pioneers embark on the Oregon Trail
- Edison's invention of the light bulb
- the first Model-T Ford takes to the road

Historical event: _____

1. Who was there? _____

2. When did it happen? _____

3. What are some details of that time in history?

   • How did people dress? _____

   _____

   • What kinds of transportation were available then? _____

   _____

   • How did people communicate over long distances? _____

   _____

4. What happened first? _____

5. What happened next? _____

6. What was the outcome? _____

   _____

B. Now, using your notes from Part A as a guide, retell a story from history. You may write your story in prose or in poetry. When you are finished, double-check the sequence of events to make sure you've followed chronological order. In addition, check for completeness. Have you left out anything important? If so, add it and write a revised version.

Prewriting: Brainstorming

Brainstorming is a useful prewriting technique. To "brainstorm," just jot down as many ideas as you can about a given topic. The goal is to loosen up and get the ideas flowing. Because several brains working together are better than just one, brainstorming often works better in a group. Or, just brainstorm yourself!

Get together with a group and have a brainstorming session. Jot down as many story ideas as possible about each of the following subjects.

1. **adventure stories**

   _____   _____
   _____   _____
   _____   _____
   _____   _____
   _____   _____

2. **science fiction**

   _____   _____
   _____   _____
   _____   _____
   _____   _____
   _____   _____

3. **sea stories**

   _____   _____
   _____   _____
   _____   _____
   _____   _____
   _____   _____

4. **coming-of-age stories (growing up)**

   _____   _____
   _____   _____
   _____   _____
   _____   _____
   _____   _____

5. **animal stories**

_____

_____

_____

_____

_____

_____

_____

_____

_____

_____

6. **historical fiction**

_____   _____

_____   _____

_____   _____

_____   _____

_____   _____

7. **mystery**

_____   _____

_____   _____

_____   _____

_____   _____

_____   _____

8. **fantasy**

_____   _____

_____   _____

_____   _____

_____   _____

_____   _____

Lesson 4 · If Animals Could Talk

If you've ever had a pet, you've probably wondered what went on in that animal's head. For example, did your dog really adore you the way he seemed to? Did your cat really feel as aloof toward you as she seemed to? If animals could talk, what do you think they might say?

Do you think these stripes make me look fat?

Suppose you visit the zoo. What do you imagine each of the animals might be saying to each other? What news would they share? What problems would they discuss? Would they talk about the old days when they were free in the wild? Write two sentences that each animal might say. Use your imagination!

1. **a zebra**

_____

_____

2. **a monkey**

_____

_____

3. **an alligator**

_____

_____

4. **a bear**

_____

_____

5. **a cobra**

_____

_____

6. **an elephant**

_____

_____

7. **a flamingo**

_____

_____

8. **a hippo**

_____

_____

9. **a koala**

_____

_____

10. **a lion**

_____

_____

11. **a rhino**

_____

_____

12. **a gazelle**

_____

_____

13. **a tiger**

_____

_____

14. **a camel**

_____

_____

Lesson 5 · Travelogue

A *travelogue* is a narrated film about a trip. In the narration that goes along with the film, the writer makes observations about the people and places being shown. The observations might include the writer's own experiences and feelings. They might also include travel tips for anyone who might want to take the same trip.

A. Think of a familiar place. It might be a place you visited on vacation or a place in your hometown that you visit frequently. It might even be a place you have never visited but have read a lot about. For some ideas, see the suggestions in the box.

Mexico	**Egypt**	**the Statue of Liberty**	**a hiking trail**
Florida	**Canada**	**the Golden Gate Bridge**	**Lake Tahoe**
Hawaii	**Vermont**	**a park near your home**	**a ski resort**
Chicago	**New York**	**the White House**	**a national park**
Seattle	**the Alamo**	**an amusement park**	**the Eiffel Tower**

1. What place is it? _____

_____

2. What is special about this place? _____

_____

_____

3. Describe what the place looks like. _____

_____

_____

4. What sounds might you hear at this place? _____

_____

5. What aromas might you smell here? _____

_____

6. Describe any special tastes that are associated with the place.

_____

7. Do you need to wear any type of special clothing here? If so, describe it.

_____

8. What kinds of photographs would a traveler be likely to take here?

_____

_____

9. What tips would you give a traveler who planned a visit to this place?

_____

_____

B. Suppose you have made a video of the place you described. Using your notes, write a travelogue to accompany it. As you write, ask yourself what a first-time traveler would want to know. Try to supply information that would be interesting and useful to a tourist.

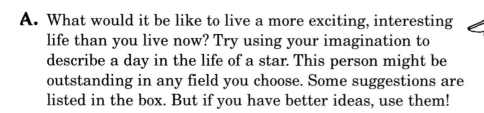

"A Day in the Life of . . ."

A. What would it be like to live a more exciting, interesting life than you live now? Try using your imagination to describe a day in the life of a star. This person might be outstanding in any field you choose. Some suggestions are listed in the box. But if you have better ideas, use them!

actor	pianist	scientific researcher	jazz musician
parent	politician	circus performer	pop singer
artist	doctor	clothing designer	racecar driver
model	opera star	CEO of a company	school principal
teacher	comedian	professional athlete	talk-show host

1. What type of work would you do? _____

2. What would you enjoy most about this kind of life? _____

    _____

3. What special duties or tasks would you have to take care of every day?
   List three things.

    _____

    _____

    _____

4. What recreation or entertainment would you enjoy as often as you could?
   List three things.

    _____

    _____

    _____

5. What would be the *best* thing about doing this kind of work? _____

    _____

    _____

6. What would be the *worst* thing about living this life? _____

    _____

    _____

7. Describe a typical morning, afternoon, and evening in your life. _____

_____

_____

_____

_____

B. Using the notes you made, write a story about a day in the person's life. You may use either a first-person point of view (I am . . .) or a third-person point of view (he or she is . . .).

Sentences: Fragments and Run-Ons

A *fragment* is part of a sentence. It does not express a complete thought, as a sentence does. A fragment might lack a subject or a predicate, or it might be a dependent clause.

The girl with the purple necklace. (lacks a predicate)
Wore a pair of sparkling red shoes. (lacks a subject)
Because she wanted to attract attention. (dependent clause)

To correct a fragment, simply add the part that is missing. Possible corrections:

The girl with the purple necklace laughed.
The dancer wore a pair of sparkling red shoes.
She dressed in bright colors because she wanted
*   to attract attention.*

A *run-on* is two or more sentences written as one sentence.

The girl with the purple necklace danced a jig she wore
*   sparkling red shoes she attracted some attention.*

To correct a run-on, join the ideas, being careful to separate them with proper punctuation. Possible corrections:

The girl with the purple necklace attracted some attention as she danced a jig in her sparkling red shoes.

The girl with the purple necklace danced a jig. She wore sparkling red shoes and attracted some attention.

Write **fragment** or **run-on** to identify each example below. Then write a corrected version of each partial sentence.

1. _____ A huge teepee.

_____

2. _____ Hundreds of paintings are on the walls the artist would have been proud.

_____

_____

3. _____ The show, which highlights the work of George Catlin.

_____

4. _____ Was exhibited at the Smithsonian American Art Museum in Washington, D.C.

_____

_____

5. _____ An incredible record of Native American culture.

_____

6. _____ Catlin portrayed American Indians as fellow human beings rather than as savages he was one of the few artists to do so.

_____

_____

_____

7. _____ Catlin's own mother had been abducted by the Iroquois in 1778 she was released unharmed.

_____

_____

8. _____ Often told her son about her experience.

_____

9. _____ Catlin showed his early portraits to General William Clark he asked for Clark's help in contacting Indians in the West.

_____

_____

_____

10. _____ At first was skeptical.

_____

11. _____ Convinced by Catlin that he was serious.

_____

12. _____ Clark took Catlin 400 miles up the Mississippi River several tribes were having a council there.

_____

_____

13. _____ Catlin began painting he was there for six years he painted 300 portraits and about 175 landscapes and ritual scenes.

_____

_____

_____

"One Thing I'll Always Remember"

A *memoir* is a narrative based on personal experience. What events from your past are especially memorable? When you write a memoir, you usually recall details about a specific event. Perhaps these are sensory details: how something looked, sounded, or tasted. Or perhaps the details involve what other people said or did.

A. Write a sentence that you might include in a memoir about each of the following topics:

1. a beloved pet _____
   _____
   _____
   _____

2. a favorite relative _____
   _____

3. a dear friend _____
   _____

4. a helpful teacher _____
   _____

5. a sporting event _____
   _____

6. learning a new skill _____
   _____

7. a turning point _____
   _____

8. a feeling of accomplishment _____
   _____

9. a disappointment _____
   _____

B. Now, choose one of the topics in Part A and develop it into a short memoir.

My topic is _____.

Before you begin, make a list of words and phrases that might answer each of the following questions about the topic:

1. What sights, sounds, or smells do I associate with this topic? _____

   _____

   _____

2. What happened? Describe the action involved. Is my recollection a single event or a series of events? _____

   _____

   _____

3. Who played a role in this memory? Describe the person or persons. _____

   _____

   _____

Write a first draft of your memoir on the lines below. When you are finished, exchange papers with a classmate. Critique each other's work, and then write a revised version on a separate sheet of paper.

Lesson 8 — Writing a Biography

A *biography* is the story of someone's life, as written by another person. Usually, events in a biography are written in chronological order, beginning with the subject's childhood. The biographer's main goal is to give an accurate impression of the subject's personality. A biography might include information about any of the following:

- the subject's ancestors
- the social climate of the time
- political events that took place during the subject's life
- letters written to and by the subject
- anecdotes, or short narratives about amusing or interesting incidents

Shedding light on your subject's personality is the sole purpose of a biography. Any information that does not contribute to this goal should be excluded. Suppose you're writing a biography of someone who lived during the Civil War, for example. The only information about the war that you would include would be those facts that directly affected your subject.

A. Choose a subject for a biography from the list below, or name anyone you like.

a relative of yours	**a pioneer**	**a famous artist**	**a president**
a famous writer	**an athlete**	**a political activist**	**a scientist**

Answer these questions about your subject:

1. What is the name of your subject? _____

2. What insight into that person's character will be the focus of your biography?

   _____

   _____

3. Will information about the person's ancestors help your reader understand
   your subject? (yes or no) _____   If so, what is that information and how
   does it help? _____

   _____

   _____

4. How was your subject educated? _____

   _____

5. How would you describe your subject's greatest accomplishment?

   _____

   _____

6. What anecdote might your subject's best friend tell about him or her?

_____

_____

7. What anecdote might your subject's mother or father tell?

_____

_____

B. Now, write a few paragraphs that would be part of your biography. You may expand on any of the answers you have already given about your subject.

Lesson 9 — Paraphrasing a Famous Fable or Folktale

When you *paraphrase*, you restate an author's ideas in different words. The purpose of paraphrasing is to share information by clarifying the meaning for readers. Here is an example:

ORIGINAL SENTENCE: *A conceited hare boasted loudly about her ability to run fast.*

PARAPHRASE: *A stuck-up rabbit bragged about how fast she could run.*

Read these lines from one version of a famous fable about two travelers and a bear. Then write a paraphrase of each sentence. The first one has been done as an example:

1. A man and his friend made their way through the forest on a narrow path.

   Two men were walking together through the woods on a lonely trail.

2. They heard the sound of heavy feet trampling through the underbrush up ahead.

   _____

   _____

3. One of them whispered in alarm, "It could be a bear!"

   _____

   _____

4. As quickly as he could, he scrambled up a tall tree, leaving his friend behind.

   _____

   _____

5. He had barely reached the first branch when a huge brown bear pushed aside the bushes and appeared on the path.

   _____

   _____

6. Holding onto the tree with both arms, the first traveler refused to help his frightened companion.

   _____

   _____

7. The second traveler, terrified, threw himself on the ground and prepared to die.

_____

_____

8. The bear lowered its huge head and sniffed at the man, mussing his hair with his nose.

_____

_____

9. Then, to the astonishment of both men, the wild animal walked away.

_____

_____

10. The first traveler came down from the tree.

_____

_____

11. In a wondering tone, he said, "It almost looked as if the bear whispered a secret into your ear."

_____

_____

12. "It did," said the second traveler. "It told me that for my next journey, I should choose a better companion."

_____

_____

_____

13. The moral of the story is this:

Misfortune is the true test of friendship.

_____

_____

_____

_____

Grammar: Parts of Speech

Recognizing parts of speech helps you use words correctly. Review these definitions:

- **noun** A word or phrase that names a person, place, thing, quality, or act

  Norman, Los Angeles, football, generosity, declaration

- **pronoun** a word that substitutes for a noun

  he, she, them

- **verb** a word or phrase that expresses action or existence

  dance, are

- **adjective** a word that modifies a noun or a pronoun

  purple, third

- **adverb** a word that modifies a verb, an adjective, or another adverb

  quickly, very, soon

- **preposition** a word or phrase that shows the relationship of a noun to a verb, an adjective, or another noun

  at, by, between

- **conjunction** a word that connects other words, phrases, or sentences

  and, but, or, because

- **interjection** a word, phrase, or sound used as an exclamation and capable of standing by itself

  gosh, my goodness!

A. Identify each underlined word's part of speech.

1. _____ Because Patrick was going on a bike trip, <u>he</u> bought supplies for three days on the road.

2. _____ He <u>packed</u> a lightweight bag and took off at dawn.

3. _____ He rode 15 miles to Eric's <u>house</u>, and the boys continued from there.

4. _____ When they got <u>to</u> the beach, they ate their lunch.

5. _____ Hours later, they arrived at the city of <u>Long Beach</u>.

6. _____ They boarded the ferry to Catalina <u>and</u> enjoyed the ride to the island.

7. _____ For <u>three</u> days, they biked around the island and slept outdoors.

8. _____ Patrick and Eric saw a buffalo up close, but they weren't <u>scared</u> of it.

9. _____ Eric had a flat tire, but he was able to fix it <u>easily</u>.

10. _____ The two friends relaxed on the beach and <u>swam</u> in the ocean.

11. _____ <u>Alas</u>! Too soon it was time to go home.

B. Write a word to complete each sentence.
Then identify the word's part of speech.

PART OF SPEECH

1. Achilles is a character _____
   Greek mythology.

   _____

2. When Achilles was an infant, his mother
   _____ him into a magical river.

   _____

3. _____ was trying to make
   her son immortal.

   _____

4. She held him by his heel, _____
   that part of his body didn't get wet.

   _____

5. After that, his heel _____ Achilles'
   only body part that could be injured.

   _____

6. When Achilles grew up, he was one of
   Greece's _____ warriors.

   _____

7. Then he was wounded in battle by an arrow
   that _____ him in the heel.

   _____

8. _____! That injury caused his death.

   _____

9. Have you _____ heard the
   expression "Achilles' heel"?

   _____

10. That _____ refers to the most
    vulnerable point in a person's character.

    _____

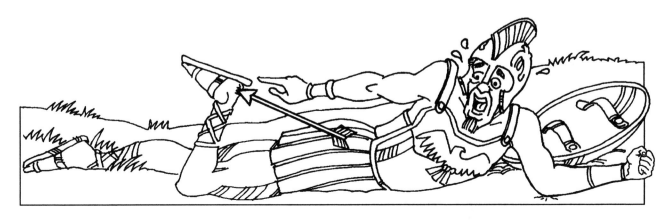

Writing a Plot for a Mystery Story

The unknown plays an important role in every mystery story. Who did it? What was that strange noise in the night? Will the detective find the scoundrel? Who (or what) has been pursuing our hero so relentlessly—and why?

As you might guess, mystery writers know the answers to such questions before they begin writing. As they write, they drop clues to the reader.

An observant reader can sometimes figure out the mystery before finishing the story. In fact, if the ending is a complete surprise, the writer has not done a good job! After finishing a mystery, the reader should be able to go back through the story and find clues that hinted at the solution.

Read the following beginning of a mystery story.

Sylvia was early for her weekly lunch date with her friend Marcy. In the hotel lobby where they planned to meet, she sat on a comfortable, deep sofa. She would enjoy the 45 minutes she had to wait by reading her book.

When she opened the book, the pencil she'd been using as a bookmark slipped out. It bounced off her leg and rolled into the crack between the sofa's arm and cushion. Sylvia squeezed her fingers into the crack to retrieve the pencil. She felt something cold and smooth, like a marble. Pulling it up, she discovered that it was a pearl ring. She examined it, delighted at its beauty.

Just as she was getting ready to turn it in at the lost-and-found desk, an old woman came up and spoke to her.

"Give me back my ring!" the woman said in a gravelly voice.

"This ring? Does it belong to you?" asked Sylvia.

"It belongs to anyone who can handle its magic," the woman said. "If you can't handle it, then give it back to me."

"What are you talking about?" Sylvia asked.

"That is a very unusual ring," the woman went on. "Why, that ring came from . . ."

Now think about how *you* would solve the mystery. Remember to give the reader a few hints along the way, so the ending isn't a complete surprise. Answer these questions before you actually write the rest of the story.

1. Who is the old woman? _____

2. What does she tell Sylvia about the origins of the ring?

_____

_____

3. Is she telling the truth about the ring? _____

4. Will Sylvia give the ring to her? _____

   If so, what happens next? _____

   _____

   If not, what happens next? _____

   _____

   _____

5. Will Sylvia's friend Marcy have
   anything to do with the rest of the story? _____

   If not, why not? _____

   _____

   If so, what will Marcy do? _____

   _____

   _____

Now, write the rest of the story. Use another sheet of paper if necessary.
When you are finished, make up a catchy title for your story.

CATCHY TITLE: _____

"That is a very unusual ring," the woman went on. "Why, that
ring came from _____

_____

_____

_____

_____

_____

_____

_____

_____

_____

_____

_____

_____

Lesson 11 — Using Setting as a Springboard

Setting—a story's time and place—is an important literary element. Details about setting often determine details about the characters and plot. For example, if a story is set in the mid-1800s, the characters won't be using cars or computers. Similarly, if a story is set in Alaska, the characters won't be spending time in bathing suits at the beach.

A. Read the following passages from well-known novels. Then, after each one, answer the questions about setting.

FROM *THE MARTIAN CHRONICLES* BY RAY BRADBURY

Outside, the immense blue Martian sky was hot and still as a warm deep sea water. The Martian desert lay broiling like a prehistoric mud pot, waves of heat rising and shimmering. There was a small rocket ship reclining upon a hilltop nearby. Large footprints came from the rocket to the door of this stone house. . . . After fifteen minutes the Earth men began walking in and out the kitchen door, with nothing to do.

---

1. Where does this story take place? _____

2. Is it the past, the present, or the future? _____

   How do you know this? _____

FROM THE SADDLEBACK ADAPTATION OF *SWISS FAMILY ROBINSON* BY JOHANN WYSS

Shipwrecked! But looking around, I saw that our position was by no means hopeless. The part of the ship that held our cabin was jammed between two high rocks. Luckily, it was partly raised above the waves. Through clouds of mist and rain, I could see a rocky, rugged coast. I told my frightened family that as soon as the storm ended, we would make our way to the shore. . . .

The storm finally ended at dawn.. . . The animals on the ship needed to be fed. They were frightened and hungry, having been neglected during the storm. The two large dogs in the captain's cabin were thrilled when Jack let them out at last. The following useful animals were also on the ship: a cow, a donkey, two goats, six sheep, a ram, and a fine pig. Then we found that we also had ten hens and two roosters, as well as some ducks, geese, and pigeons.

---

3. Describe the setting of this scene. _____

   _____

4. What details suggest that this story takes place in the past? _____

   _____

   _____

> **FROM THE SADDLEBACK ADAPTATION OF *THE RED BADGE OF COURAGE* BY STEPHEN CRANE**
>
> A cloud of fog rose slowly from the cold earth. The rising sun revealed a camp of Union army soldiers stretched out on the hills. Last night the Yankees had seen the red gleam of enemy campfires on a distant hillside. Today, they were hoping for some action.

5. What is the setting of this story? _____

6. How do you know this? _____

B. Try your own hand at establishing setting in a paragraph. Use clues about time and place to help your reader visualize the scene. You may choose from the following settings, or use an idea of your own.

- a cowboy town of the Old West
- an African village in 2004
- a California gold-mining town in 1849
- a Southern plantation in 1860
- a battlefield in World War I

- Paris in the 1920s
- Los Angeles in 2992
- when dinosaurs lived
- a future emergency room
- modern New York City

Lesson 12 Creating Characters

Good writers make their characters seem like real people. To accomplish this goal, they often write character descriptions based on actual people. Then, by using adjectives that appeal to all the senses, writers artfully bring their fictional characters to life.

A. Read the following example of a character description.

THE OPENING PARAGRAPH OF *LORD JIM* BY JOSEPH CONRAD

He was an inch, perhaps two, under six feet, powerfully built, and he advanced straight at you with a slight stoop of the shoulders, head forward, and a fixed from-under stare which made you think of a charging bull. His voice was deep, loud, and his manner displayed a kind of dogged self-assertion which had nothing aggressive in it. It seemed a necessity, and it was directed apparently as much at himself as at anybody else. He was spotlessly neat, apparelled in immaculate white from shoes to hat, and in the various Eastern ports where he got his living as ship-chandler's water-clerk, he was very popular.

Notice the adjectives that appeal to your sense of sight and hearing. You can create characters just as interesting as Lord Jim. How? Develop descriptions that make it easy for the reader to visualize the character. You might begin by writing lists of adjectives from which to choose. Try it!

To complete the chart, write six adjectives to describe each character.

yourself	a family member	a good friend
_____	_____	_____
_____	_____	_____
_____	_____	_____
_____	_____	_____
_____	_____	_____
_____	_____	_____

a neighbor	a co-worker	a pet
_____	_____	_____
_____	_____	_____
_____	_____	_____
_____	_____	_____
_____	_____	_____
_____	_____	_____

B. Now choose one of the characters from the chart. Write a paragraph describing the character. Be sure to use some of the adjectives you've listed.

_____

_____

_____

_____

_____

_____

_____

_____

_____

C. Read the character descriptions below. Then build on each description by adding more detail.

1. Not quite five feet tall, Señora Carlotta had a flat, brown, deeply wrinkled face framed by a halo of fine, white hair. Her eyes, black and shiny as satin, flashed with youth and strength. Knotted over her fragile, bony shoulders was a shabby shawl, which covered her shapeless cotton dress.

   _____

   _____

   _____

   _____

   _____

2. Theodore's mother was a tall blonde woman with whale-gray eyes that matched her son's. Her smile was as dazzling as the diamonds that sparkled on her ears and hands whenever she moved. Her pearl-gray cashmere sweater and silk skirt matched her elegant shoes perfectly.

   _____

   _____

   _____

   _____

Mechanics: Spelling

Spelling errors always suggest that the writer is careless. To avoid giving this impression, check a dictionary if you're not sure of a word's spelling.

A. Read each pair of words. If both words are spelled correctly, write *correct* on the line. If either or both words are spelled incorrectly, rewrite them correctly on the line.

1. busy
   building

   among
   yung

8. pillow
   velvit

   monster
   frantick

2. enuff
   straight

   though
   rough

9. appron
   local

   motive
   famous

3. eighth
   sistem

   couraje
   although

10. healed
    wundered

    bragged
    threatened

4. boulder
   dough

   biskit
   freind

11. important
    intelligence

    entrance
    presence

5. mischief
   foreign

   pier
   belief

12. statement
    argument

    activvity
    majority

6. seashoar
   upright

   cupboard
   thunderstorm

13. comercial
    commander

    committee
    confusing

7. citys
   supplies

   mummies
   enemys

14. occured
    conceit

    relieve
    column

B. Circle the one misspelled word in each sentence. Write it correctly on the line.

1. The sumit of Mount Everest is 29,035 feet above sea level.

   _____

2. On May 29, 1953, two men compleated climbing the mountain.

   _____

3. The first assent of Mount Everest was a big news story.

   _____

4. The mountain stands on one of the earth's fronteers.

   _____

5. It is part of a range that seperates Tibet and India.

   _____

6. The expadition that first climbed Everest was British.

   _____

7. Earlier attemts had been made on the Tibet side.

   _____

8. After World War II, Tibet was closed to foriegners.

   _____

9. Climbers now approatched Everest from Nepal, to the south.

   _____

10. A large group of Sherpa porters was recrooted in Nepal.

    _____

11. Tenzing Norgay, the Sherpa leader, had an elegent manner.

    _____

12. Edmund Hillary had lerned to climb in the New Zealand Alps.

    _____

13. Nobody was killed or injurred on the 1953 climb.

    _____

14. In those days, climbing mountains was an amatuer occupation.

    _____

15. Today, people climb Everest on comercially run adventures.

    _____

Lesson 13 — Dialogue

Dialogue is conversation between story characters. The way characters speak and the words they use make them "real" to the reader. When you write dialogue, you can reveal a lot about a character's personality, attitudes, and level of education.

As you read the dialogue in the box to the right, notice the following points:

- Quotation marks set off a speaker's exact words.

- The first word of a quotation is capitalized.

- Each new speaker gets a new paragraph.

- Words that explain who is speaking go outside the quotation marks.

> "I'm having a party on Friday," Marsha said, "and I'd like you to come."
>
> Jacob looked sadly at Marsha and said, "I already have plans for Friday. I'm so sorry I'll have to miss the event."
>
> "Oh, Jacob, I'm so disappointed," Marsha replied. "Maybe next time?"
>
> "I'll look forward to it," Jacob said. "Your parties are always so much fun."

A. Try writing your own dialogue, making sure to use correct form. For ideas, choose from the suggestions in the box.

Ideas for People	Ideas for Topics	
a brother and a sister	a school project	a movie
a grandparent and a grandchild	a situation at home	an invention
a teacher and a student	future plans	a book
a parent and a child	the weather	an election
two friends	a news event	fashion
an employer and an employee	an argument	a vacation
you and your favorite performer	an athletic event	a new job
two enemies	an upcoming test	a concert

Begin your dialogue here, and continue it on the next page.

_____

_____

_____

_____

_____

_____

_____

_____

_____

_____

_____

_____

B. Now, write a dialogue to continue the following conversation. You may include as many characters as you want. Just make sure that each one can be recognized as a separate voice. Try to reveal differences in your characters by what they say and how they say it.

"The train is leaving in ten minutes!" Laura exclaimed. "Hurry!"
Sam, bored as usual, answered, "What's the big deal? I don't even want to go."

_____

_____

_____

_____

_____

_____

_____

_____

_____

_____

_____

_____

_____

_____

_____

Conflicts in a Narrative

Every story has a *conflict* (problem or struggle) of some kind. Without a conflict, there is no story. Watching the characters work out that conflict keeps a reader interested. A story conflict can be between two people, between a person and some outside force, or within a single character's mind. Read these examples of conflicts:

CONFLICT BETWEEN TWO PEOPLE

Claire spends weekends at her dad's house, sharing a room with her stepsister Jane. The two girls don't get along at all. Claire is a serious student who works hard to stay on top of her school assignments. All Jane thinks about is keeping up with the latest styles in clothing and music. Jane thinks Claire is boring, and Claire thinks Jane is empty-headed.

CONFLICT BETWEEN A PERSON AND AN OUTSIDE FORCE

Robert is going to his family's cabin in the mountains for the weekend. He wants to go skiing. He also plans to stock the cabin with food and other essentials for the rest of the winter. But the first night, snow falls so heavily that he can't even open the door in the morning! He is snowed in, and he hasn't had time to buy groceries yet! Robert has only enough food for one more day.

CONFLICT WITHIN A PERSON'S OWN MIND

Gloria has been invited to the wedding of one of her best friends. Unfortunately, the wedding will take place on the same day as her grandparents' 50th wedding anniversary. A big party is planned for the anniversary, and Gloria is expected to attend. Everyone else in the family will be there, including relatives who live 3,000 miles away. Gloria is torn between the wedding and the anniversary party.

A. Read the following situations. Decide whether or not each one is a conflict. Write *conflict* or *no conflict* after each situation.

1. Joyce buys a new pair of boots, and Sunny buys a cool pair of jeans. Later, the two friends have lunch and admire each other's purchases. _____

2. Albert and Frankie are both interested in Selena. Each boy tells Selena bad things about the other. Selena doesn't know what to think. _____

3. Stuart needs better grades to get into college. He heard he can get an "easy A" in music appreciation. But that class won't help him pass the college entrance exam. _____

B. Now, write your own examples of conflicts. If you like, write about an actual experience. Perhaps you were once in a dangerous situation or competed with someone. If not, you may write about an imaginary situation.

CONFLICT BETWEEN TWO PEOPLE

CONFLICT BETWEEN A PERSON AND AN OUTSIDE FORCE

CONFLICT WITHIN A PERSON'S OWN MIND

Lesson 15 — Climax

The *climax* of a story is the point at which the conflict is resolved. All the action in the story builds toward this moment. The part of a story leading up to the climax is called the *rising action*. The part after the climax is called the *falling action*.

Sometimes a story's climax is a surprise to the reader. But remember that a story with a surprise ending should not come as a *complete* surprise. Hints should appear somewhere in the story to give the reader clues. The ending has to be consistent with the characters and how they would act.

King Midas was a kind but foolish man who lived in Greece long ago. One day, in exchange for a kindness, he was granted a wish. Without thinking of the consequences of his wish, King Midas asked that everything he touched would turn to gold. The "golden touch," as it was called, made him very rich.

Unfortunately, however, even his food and drink turned to gold. He could not eat or drink. But the worst thing was what happened when his daughter ran to hug him. She, too, turned to gold! Finally, King Midas begged to have his golden touch removed. When he was granted this second wish, his daughter was restored to life.

A. Read the story above and then answer the following questions:

1. Who is the main character? _____

2. What is the conflict in this story? _____

_____

_____

_____

3. What is the climax of the story? _____

_____

_____

B. Now, take notes for an original story.

1. Write a sentence describing the conflict. _____

   _____

   _____

2. List the characters, and give a brief description of each one.

   _____

   _____

   _____

   _____

3. Write a brief outline of the events (both before and after the climax).

   _____

   _____

   _____

   _____

   _____

   _____

4. Write a sentence telling how the conflict will be resolved. _____

   _____

   _____

Begin your story here. Use additional sheets of paper as necessary.
Write a first draft, then edit it. Next, trade stories with a classmate,
asking for suggestions for improvement. Then, make a final copy of
your story, and share it by reading it aloud.

_____

_____

_____

_____

_____

_____

_____

Vocabulary

A good *vocabulary* is a basic requirement for good writing. One of the best ways to increase your vocabulary is by using a dictionary to look up unfamiliar words. Dictionary entries also include word pronunciations and, often, origins of words. Many dictionaries also suggest synonyms and antonyms.

A. Use a dictionary to find the meaning of each word. Write the definition on the first line. Then, use the word in a sentence of your own on the second line.

1. **astute** _____
   _____

2. **commodity** _____
   _____

3. **effigy** _____
   _____

4. **grandiose** _____
   _____

5. **inducement** _____
   _____

6. **consensus** _____
   _____

7. **jargon** _____
   _____

8. **oblivious** _____
   _____

9. **quire** _____
   _____

10. **expatriate** _____
    _____

11. **umbrage** _____
    _____

12. **chivalry** _____
    _____

Another tool for improving your vocabulary is a *thesaurus*. Instead of definitions, word origins, and pronunciations, a thesaurus lists synonyms for words. In some cases, a thesaurus will also list antonyms for words.

B. Here are two thesaurus entries for the word *increase*. Choose eight of the synonyms given for *increase*, and write a sentence using each one.

increase *n.* development, spread, swell, enlargement, expansion, escalation, boost, elaboration, swelling, addition, incorporation, merger, inflation, heightening, extension, dilation, multiplication, deepening, hike, amplification, progression, improvement, jump, boom.
—*Ant.* reduction, decline, decrease.

increase *v.* extend, enlarge, expand, dilate, broaden, widen, thicken, deepen, heighten, build, lengthen, magnify, add on, augment, escalate, let out, branch out, further, mark up, sharpen, build up, raise, enhance, amplify, reinforce, supplement, annex, double, triple, stretch, multiply, intensify, prolong, exaggerate, redouble, boost, step up, rev up.
—*Ant.* decrease, reduce, abridge.

1. _____

_____

2. _____

_____

3. _____

_____

4. _____

_____

5. _____

_____

6. _____

_____

7. _____

_____

8. _____

_____

Lesson 16 — Tone and Mood

Tone and *mood* are related terms. When you write a narrative, your voice expresses a certain tone, or attitude, toward your subject. Your tone might be formal or informal, serious or playful. It may be somber, ironic, condescending, intimate, sad, thoughtful, or one of many other possible attitudes. The writer's tone creates an overall feeling or atmosphere in the story.

The following paragraphs are about the same subject—a young person leaving home. Notice the different tone and mood as you read each paragraph.

Full of bitterness and dark thoughts, young Samuel trudged on and on. The diner up ahead made only a dim glow against the gray background of twilight. Beyond the diner, almost as far as the horizon, he could see the railway station on a small hill. He wept with sorrow and regret to be leaving this place, his home for the past seven years.

Her heart fluttering with excitement, Arielle skipped, nearly dancing, toward the diner. Its cheerful light gleamed in the dusk. Somehow it seemed like a symbol of hope for her future. Farther on, she could see the railway station on the hill. How delighted she was to be leaving this place, her home for the past seven years.

A. 1. Write five words from the first paragraph that contribute to the sorrowful tone.

_____

2. Write five words of your own that the author *could* have used to create a sorrowful tone.

_____

3. Write five words from the second paragraph that contribute to the joyful tone.

_____

4. Write five words of your own that the author *could* have used to create a joyful tone.

_____

B. Now, write two paragraphs of your own, using different tones to describe similar scenes or situations. Ideas for topics and tones are in the box. Choose one topic and two tones. If you prefer, you may use your own topic and your own ideas for two different tones.

Possible Topics	**Possible Tones**		
getting a new hairstyle	compassionate	regretful	joyful
discovering a new insect	wondering	ashamed	angry
buying a pair of sunglasses	humorous	sorrowful	tender
getting caught in a tornado	horror-stricken	delighted	proud
hiking in a wilderness area	desperate	resentful	ironic
going deep-sea fishing	disappointed	worried	informal
going to a Renaissance fair	awe-inspiring	fearful	confused
inventing a time-saver	respectful	formal	frightened

■ _____

_____

_____

_____

_____

_____

_____

_____

_____

■ _____

_____

_____

_____

_____

_____

_____

_____

Good writing has *style*. Like style in clothing fashions, writing style expresses a person's individuality. Word choice, sentence structure and variety, and rhythm are all part of a writer's style. Imagery, emphasis, and arrangement of ideas are also contributing factors.

Notice the different styles in these two passages:

FROM *THE CALL OF THE WILD* BY JACK LONDON

From every hill slope came the trickle of running water, the music of unseen fountains. All things were thawing, bending, snapping. The Yukon was straining to break loose the ice that bound it down. It ate away from beneath; the sun ate from above. Air holes formed, fissures sprang apart, while thin sections of ice fell through bodily into the river. And amid all this bursting, rending, throbbing of awakening life, under the blazing sun and through the soft-sighing breezes, like wayfarers to death, staggered the two men, the woman, and the huskies.

FROM *THE HOBBIT* BY J.R.R. TOLKIEN

They had not been riding very long when up came Gandalf very splendid on a white horse. He had brought a lot of pocket-handkerchiefs, and Bilbo's pipe and tobacco. So after that the party went along very merrily, and they told stories or sang songs as they rode forward all day, except of course when they stopped for meals. These didn't come quite as often as Bilbo would have liked them, but still he began to feel that adventures were not so bad after all.

Both passages are based on the travels of a group of characters. In the first example, the author emphasizes the surroundings, describing nature in quite poetic terms. In the second, the author emphasizes what the characters are doing and how they feel about it.

Try your own hand at writing in different styles. Follow the suggestions below.

1. Write a paragraph describing the seasonal changes that take place in nature. Try to use a poetic style, full of sensory imagery, as in the first example.

_____

_____

_____

_____

_____

_____

2. Write a paragraph describing a group of friends on a trip. They might be walking, driving, riding bikes, or whatever you wish. Use a merry, lighthearted style, as in the second example.

_____

_____

_____

_____

_____

_____

_____

3. Write a paragraph explaining a familiar scientific concept (e.g., evaporation, gravity, etc.). Write in a straightforward, explanatory manner similar to the style used in a science book or an encyclopedia.

_____

_____

_____

_____

_____

_____

_____

4. Write a paragraph describing a funny incident that happened to you or to someone you know. Use a humorous style that seems appropriate to the story.

_____

_____

_____

_____

_____

_____

_____

How does an idea for a TV show or movie get from the writer's brain to the screen? The process involves a series of steps resulting in a *script*. A script is the written version of the idea, complete with directions for camera angles, lighting, and acting. It might also include descriptions of sets and costumes. To describe camera shots, writers use abbreviations such as INT., for interior, and EXT., for exterior, to show where the scene takes place.

As you read the example on the right, notice the following points:

- The name of the speaker is printed in **boldface**.

- Actors' stage directions are printed in *italics* and enclosed in parentheses.

- Camera directions are printed in capital letters and set off from the dialogue.

> **Bertha:** He gave away the money, Andrew.
>
> **Andrew:** Who gave away what money?
>
> **Bertha:** The insurance money. William gave it all away.
>
> **Andrew** *(in disbelief)*: No! He *gave* it away?
>
> **Bertha:** He would tell you that he made an investment. But he made it with a man even a dog wouldn't have trusted.
>
> CUT TO:
>
> INT.--WILLIAM IN BEDROOM, LISTENING
>
> **Andrew** *(offscreen)*: And the money is gone?
>
> **Bertha** *(offscreen)*: Gone. All of it.

Write your own scene for a video script. For your scene, choose a memorable day in your life. It could be winning a game, a family event, or a time you received good news or bad news. Feel free to make up details and add new characters to make the scene more interesting.

Before you begin, outline your scene by answering these questions:

1. What happened?

   _____

2. Who was involved?

   _____

3. Where did it take place?

   _____

   _____

   _____

   _____

Begin by developing your characters in your own mind. Remember that a writer reveals the characters' personalities through their dialogue and actions as well as by the comments and actions of other characters. Complete a chart like this one for *each* character in your scene. Choose details that help you imagine how each character looks, sounds, and behaves.

Character's name: _____ Age: _____
Male or female: _____ Hair: _____ Eyes: _____
Physical type: _____ Personality: _____
Clothes: _____
Favorite foods: _____
Favorite activities: _____
What character wants: _____
What character dislikes: _____

Now write appropriate dialogue between your characters. Be aware that conversational language may include slang, contractions, and incomplete sentences. Include stage and camera directions about actors' delivery, settings, costumes, and movements.

Begin your video script here. Use additional sheets of paper as necessary to complete your first draft. Then, trade scripts with a classmate and discuss different dialogue options for each character. Use another sheet of paper for your final copy.

_____

_____

_____

_____

_____

_____

_____

_____

_____

_____

Modifiers: Adjectives and Adverbs

Choosing vivid adjectives and adverbs is an effective way to make your writing livelier. Review these definitions and examples:

- **Adjectives** modify nouns and pronouns. They can make ideas clearer by telling which one, what kind, or how many.

  the *first* contestant   a *sweet* peach   *fourteen* turtles

- **Adverbs** modify verbs, adjectives, and other adverbs. They can make ideas clearer by telling how, when, where, how often, or to what extent.

  danced *gracefully*   arrived *tonight*   drove *there*   *very* sincere

Rewrite each of the following sentences. Add at least one adjective and one adverb to make the ideas clearer. Then, identify each adjective and adverb and tell what it does.

EXAMPLE:

The alarm clock buzzed.

The dependable alarm clock buzzed loudly. dependable: adjective telling what kind; loudly: adverb telling how

1. Devon thought of a photograph he had seen.

   _____

   _____

   _____

2. The picture was of a mother and her children.

   _____

   _____

   _____

3. The woman had lost her husband.

   _____

   _____

   _____

4. The children were hungry.

_____

_____

_____

5. The photo gave an impression of the Great Depression era.

_____

_____

_____

6. A photographer can reveal information about a time in history.

_____

_____

_____

7. The farmers facing a drought had terrible problems.

_____

_____

_____

8. Loss of a farm could bring disaster to a family.

_____

_____

_____

9. The spirit of the people shines through the photograph.

_____

_____

_____

10. Pictures can speak louder than words.

_____

_____

_____

Sometimes a writer or filmmaker produces a *sequel*, or a continuation of a popular story. Why? Readers and filmgoers often become attached to a good story's characters. They wonder what might happen to them next.

A. Most books or movies do *not* have a sequel, of course. Here's your chance to brainstorm ideas for a sequel to one of your favorite books or movies.

First, make a list of your favorite books, stories, or movies. List at least six titles.

1. _____
2. _____
3. _____
4. _____
5. _____
6. _____

Now, go back and circle the one title you think should be followed with a sequel. List the most important characters, and write a brief description of each one's personality.

1. _____
2. _____
3. _____
4. _____

What do you think each character might do next?

1. _____
2. _____
3. _____
4. _____

What *new* characters might be introduced into the sequel? Name and describe them.

1. _____
2. _____
3. _____
4. _____

B. Now use your imagination to write a summary of a possible sequel. Briefly list the main events in the continuing story. Mention each character's participation in the developing plot. Pretend that you're trying to get a contract from a publisher or a film studio. Your goal is to make your sequel seem interesting and exciting enough for someone else to want to pay for it.

_____
_____
_____
_____
_____
_____
_____
_____
_____
_____
_____
_____
_____
_____
_____
_____
_____
_____
_____
_____
_____

Fast Forward

Many people have what they call a "five-year plan." That means they picture where they want to be in five years and then make plans to achieve that goal. It's also useful for young people to picture where they will be in 25 years!

A. Answer these questions about yourself, 25 years in the future.

1. How old will you be then? How will your appearance have changed?

   _____

   _____

2. What will you be doing for a living? _____

   _____

3. Will you be married or single? What will your partner be like?

   _____

   _____

   _____

4. Will you be a parent? _____ If so, what are your children's names and how old are they? _____

   _____

5. Where will you be living? Describe your residence and tell where it is located.

   _____

   _____

   _____

6. Outside of work, what will be your main interests or hobbies?_____

   _____

7. What about your parents, siblings, and other family members? Describe your future relationship with them. _____

   _____

   _____

   _____

8. What will your friends be like? Name and describe two friends in your future.

   _____

   _____

   _____

   _____

9. What will you be doing for exercise? Describe your activities.

   _____

   _____

B. Based on your answers about your future, write two diary entries you might write in 25 years.

Dear Diary: *Date:* _____

_____

_____

_____

_____

_____

_____

Dear Diary: *Date:* _____

_____

_____

_____

_____

_____

_____

What do you think inanimate objects might say if they could speak? Imagine for a moment that you are an inanimate object such as a golden ring, an old flag, or a city street. How would you see the world? What would happen to you from day to day? What kinds of changes might you see over a very long period of time?

Write an historical narrative from the point of view of four inanimate objects. Write what each object might say about its experiences. Use the first-person point of view. (That means you will refer to yourself with the pronouns *I, me, my,* and *mine.*)

1. What might a dollar bill say about all the places it's been and the different people it's seen?

_____

_____

_____

_____

_____

_____

_____

_____

_____

_____

2. How would an old house respond if asked about its history?

_____

_____

_____

_____

_____

_____

_____

_____

_____

_____

3. What would a big tree say about the people and animals who have enjoyed its shade, fruit, and foliage?

_____

_____

_____

_____

_____

_____

_____

_____

_____

_____

_____

_____

_____

_____

_____

_____

_____

_____

_____

_____

_____

4. If you asked a small neighborhood store about its history, what would it say?

_____

_____

_____

_____

_____

_____

_____

_____

_____

_____

The Writing Process: Transitional Words and Phrases

A *transition* is the process of moving or changing from one thing to another. When you write a paragraph, you move from one sentence to the next. Skillful writers use transitional words and phrases to join their sentences. Of course, you won't be using transitional words and phrases in *every* sentence. You use them only when they are necessary for a smooth flow of ideas.

Here's a list of some transitional words and phrases you can use in your writing. You might be able to think of many more.

─ TO SHOW LOGICAL RELATIONSHIPS ─

another	thus	on the other hand	for this reason	in addition
as a result	but	most importantly	for example	however
even so	also	in comparison	furthermore	although
in fact	unlike	nevertheless	in like manner	similarly
at least	despite	in the same way	in conclusion	therefore
indeed	because	most of all	on the contrary	consequently

─ TO SHOW TIME RELATIONSHIPS ─

at first	then	next	some time later	at last
shortly	as	a little later	that afternoon	afterward
earlier	later	as long as	at the same time	as soon as
until	now	meanwhile	during that time	one morning
finally	soon	after that	immediately	before long

Rewrite each pair of sentences, using a transitional word or phrase to make the meaning clearer. You may combine the sentences into one or keep them separate. If you need to, add or change some words to make the sentences flow smoothly.

1. Danielle decided to become physically fit. She joined a gym.

   _____

   _____

2. George did not really enjoy gyms. He joined Danielle's gym.

   _____

   _____

3. The gym offered aerobics classes. It offered yoga classes.

_____

_____

4. Danielle was interested in yoga. She attended a few classes.

_____

_____

5. Danielle practiced yoga for several months. She lifted weights.

_____

_____

6. George signed up for yoga. He didn't enjoy it.

_____

_____

7. He thought yoga was boring. He thought basketball was fun.

_____

_____

8. Danielle enjoyed swimming. George did not.

_____

_____

9. Lynne was an excellent yoga instructor.
   She emphasized the importance of concentration.

   _____

   _____

   _____

10. George thought Lynne's class was silly.
    He thought the weight room was
    much more useful.

    _____

    _____

    _____

Final Project

Eyewitness Account: The First Thanksgiving

Follow these steps to write an eyewitness account of an important event:

1. **Prewriting: Choose a point of view.**

   An eyewitness account will, of course, be written from the first-person point of view. The person telling the story will use the pronouns *I*, *me*, *my*, *mine*, and *myself*. Consider these questions:

   • Do you want to tell the story of the first Thanksgiving from the point of view of a Pilgrim or a Native American?

   • Will your speaker be a child or an adult?

   • Will your speaker be male or female?

   • What will be your speaker's role in the first Thanksgiving?

   Describe your speaker here:

   _____

   _____

   _____

   _____

   _____

   _____

2. **Prewriting: Gathering Details**

   Before you write your first draft, gather details for your eyewitness account. Use a variety of sources, such as history books, art, online encyclopedias, the Internet, and so on. You might also want to interview someone with special knowledge about the subject, such as a history teacher. Take notes on separate note cards, identifying the source of the information. Be sure to take accurate and careful notes. Why? You might need to cite the source in footnotes and a bibliography.

3. Prewriting: Organizing Information

Now, organize your cards into sections of related information. As you read through your cards, ask yourself how your eyewitness will be affected by the information. For example, if your eyewitness is an adult Pilgrim female, her job might have been to prepare pies for the feast. Does your information provide details about the kinds of pies that were served or the way they were baked? If necessary, eliminate notes that do not apply to your eyewitness's point of view.

You may want to incorporate the point of view of another character by adding dialogue. For example, suppose your eyewitness is a Native American boy. He might have a conversation with an adult Pilgrim. This would add more than a one-dimensional view to your account.

4. Drafting

After organizing your notes, you can begin a first draft of your eyewitness account. Follow these tips as you write:

• Keep your eyewitness in mind. How would he or she view the events of the day?

• Refer to your note cards for accurate information.

• Get your ideas down on paper quickly. Don't worry about every little detail of mechanics. You can polish your work later.

• Write a strong opening to capture the reader's attention.

• Now develop the body of your story by working in the information you have gathered. You can use facts about the participants, menu, weather, and so on.

• Use your imagination to add dialogue that is consistent with the facts.

• Write an effective conclusion. You might end with some strong dialogue, a prediction made by the eyewitness, or an inspiring observation about the day.

5. Revising and Editing

Carefully review your work. Look for areas that need improvement, and begin to revise. Ask yourself questions like these:

• Is it clear who the eyewitness is?

• Does the entire account sound as if it were seen through one person's eyes?

• Does the style of the writing suit the audience?

• Is the body of your account well-organized?

• Within paragraphs in the body, are all topic sentences clear and well-supported by details?

• Can transitional words and phrases be added to improve the flow of the story?

6. Give your narrative to a peer and invite him or her to review it.

Offer to do the same for your classmate. By offering and accepting input, both of you will improve your chances of writing a good story!

7. Proofread your work.

Make sure that the spelling, grammar, and mechanics are correct. These kinds of mistakes can be distracting to your reader.

8. Make a final copy and publish it.

You can "publish" your eyewitness account in a variety of ways. Here are some ideas:

• Read your paper orally.

• Before a small group, act out the events described in your eyewitness account.

• Post a copy on a bulletin board in the classroom, or an electronic bulletin board.

• Write an e-mail to your friends, attaching a copy of your eyewitness account.